JESUS AND THE HOPE OF *His* *Coming*

TIM LAHAYE

JERRY B. JENKINS

HARVEST HOUSE PUBLISHERS

EUGENE, OREGON

232.9
LAH

Jesus and the Hope of His Coming

Copyright © 2004 by Tim LaHaye and Jerry B. Jenkins
Published by Harvest House Publishers
Eugene, Oregon 97402
www.harvesthousepublishers.com

Library of Congress Cataloging-in-Publication Data
    LaHaye, Tim F.
      Jesus and the hope of his coming / Tim LaHaye and Jerry B. Jenkins.
        p. cm.
      ISBN 0-7369-1244-4 (Hardcover)
    1. Second Advent. I. Jenkins, Jerry B. II. Title.
    BT886.3.L34 2004
    236'.9—dc22   2003014853

Published in association with Z Strategies, Inc., San Diego, CA.

Cover and design by Koechel Peterson & Associates, Inc., Minneapolis, Minnesota

Harvest House Publishers has made every effort to trace the ownership of all poems and quotes. In the event of a question arising from the use of a poem or quote, we regret any error made and will be pleased to make the necessary correction in future editions of this book.

Unless otherwise indicated, all Scripture quotations are taken from the New King James Version. Copyright © 1982 by Thomas Nelson, Inc. Used by permission. All rights reserved. Verses marked NIV are taken from the HOLY BIBLE, NEW INTERNATIONAL VERSION®. NIV®. Copyright © 1973, 1978, 1984 by the International Bible Society. Used by permission of Zondervan. All rights reserved. Verses marked NLT are taken from the *Holy Bible,* New Living Translation, copyright © 1996. Used by permission of Tyndale House Publishers, Inc., Wheaton, IL 60189 USA. All rights reserved. Verses marked NASB are taken from the New American Standard Bible®, © 1960, 1962, 1963, 1968, 1971, 1972, 1973, 1975, 1977 by The Lockman Foundation. Used by permission. (www.Lockman.org) Verses marked KJV are taken from the King James Version of the Bible.

Printed in China.

   04   05   06   07   08   09   10   11   / RDS-CF /   10   9   8   7   6   5   4   3   2   1

BRINGING TOMORROW'S HOPE INTO TODAY

Hope is such a powerful thing. It makes us look ahead with anticipation and optimism. It causes us to remain positive even when our circumstances don't look so good. Having a hopeful perspective on life, then, is good for us.

But did you know there are two kinds of hope?

First is the hope for a favorable outcome, but there's no promise it will happen. For example, we might hope that we win a contest. Or that a certain team will win a game. Or that we'll get a specific gift for our birthday. Or that we'll get a great parking spot at the mall. This kind of hope, of course, offers no assurance. It comes with no guarantees—in fact, it's speculative. There's a chance you'll be disappointed.

Then there's the hope we have as Christians. It's a hope that looks forward to the return of Jesus, first to rapture His church, and then to set up His perfect kingdom on earth. And in that kingdom, we have much to look forward to—permanent peace, true joy, and life everlasting. This hope is not speculative. All the tremendous blessings God has promised for our future *will* happen. They're guaranteed.

Many Christians don't realize is that God's plans for our future are rich with encouragement for our lives *right now!* That's what is so wonderful about Christ's second coming. It's connected not only with future benefits for us, but present-day ones as well.

Our prayer is that you'll be blessed as you discover more about the exciting—and guaranteed!—hope that awaits you...and how that hope can enrich you today.

Tim LaHaye
Jerry B. Jenkins

CONTENTS

We should live soberly, righteously,
and godly in the present age,
looking for the blessed hope and
glorious appearing of our great God
and Savior Jesus Christ.

TITUS 2:13

Perhaps Today

*I am daily waiting for
the coming of the Son of God.*

George Whitefield

Whenever God speaks, it's important for us to pay attention. And whenever God repeats Himself again and again, we should *really* sit up and take notice. That's because He's trying to tell us something He doesn't want us to miss.

With that in mind, did you know the second coming of Jesus Christ is mentioned 318 times in the New Testament? And that 28 percent of the Bible is dedicated to prophecy?

For more perspective, consider this: There are over 100 prophecies in the Bible about Jesus' first coming. If God has given us *triple* that number of prophecies about the second coming in the New Testament alone, wouldn't you say He wants us to take notice?

The second coming is the second most-dominant theme in the New Testament (the first is the doctrine of salvation by grace through faith). It's mentioned in almost all the New Testament books, sometimes extensively. One verse out of every 30 points to the second coming, or Jesus' glorious appearing.

> Never water down the Word of God, but preach it in its undiluted sternness. There must be unflinching faithfulness to the Word of God, but when you come to personal dealings with others, remember who you are—you are not some special being created in heaven, but a sinner saved by grace.
>
> OSWALD CHAMBERS

If the second coming is that important to God, then it should be important to us, too.

Jerry and I find it fascinating that the earliest Christians lived by and taught the second coming. They knew of Christ's promise to return and took it seriously—so much so that they turned the world upside down in their passion to introduce people to salvation in Christ before He returned. By A.D. 313, Christianity was so pervasive that Constantine made it the state religion of the Roman Empire. The truth of the second coming really motivated those early Christians!

You see, the early Christians knew without a doubt Christ would come back. He promised to do so. More importantly, they knew He could come at any time—that His return is imminent. Though centuries have since passed and Christ has not yet returned, His coming is still imminent. That means it could happen any day. It was the imminency of Christ's return that infused the early church with a great sense of zeal and urgency. Considering that we today are so much closer to the second coming, we should have an even greater sense of zeal and urgency!

If you knew Christ was going to return within weeks, wouldn't it affect your list of priorities in life? Wouldn't it compel you to share the gospel more freely with unbelievers you know? And wouldn't you be more motivated toward holy living? In a nutshell, prophecies about the second coming motivate us toward...

- a greater personal purity
- a more fervent sharing of the good news
- a more passionate enthusiasm for world missions

When we as Christians pay attention to the Bible's teachings about the second coming, there's a definite impact on our lives. And that's what God wants. That's a big part of why He tells us about the second coming again and again.

I (Tim) love the perspective of M. R. DeHaan, a former medical doctor who nearly died from excessive drinking before he became a Christian at age 36. In time, he became an avid teacher of Bible prophecy and he founded *Radio Bible Class*, which became a "Scripture school" for millions of listeners. Back when I was a young preacher looking for good sermon material for my little country congregation, I came across Dr. DeHaan's book *The Second Coming of Christ*. I preached from the book, and it had a profound influence on me. It molded my thinking on prophecy, evangelism, and sanctification for over five decades and gave me a worldwide missionary vision.

Years later I had the opportunity to visit the *Radio Bible Class* ministry offices in Grand Rapids, Michigan, and see Dr. DeHaan's study. What impressed me most was not his great library but a single plaque that seemed to radiate truth from his bookshelf. In large black letters, it read; PERHAPS TODAY.

Dr. DeHaan looked forward with anticipation to Christ's return. He knew it could happen at any time, and that affected how he lived. Our hope is that through this book, you'll come to have that same anticipation, and that you'll come to live every day as if it were the day of Christ's coming.

Are you looking forward to the future?

And are you letting it influence how you live right now?

You can, by remembering just two words: Perhaps today.

*In My Father's house are
many mansions; if it were not so,
I would have told you. I go
to prepare a place for you.
And if I go to prepare a place
for you, I will come again
and receive you to Myself;
that where I am,
there you may be also.*

JOHN 14:2-3

Promises You
Can Count On

Christ is the fulfiller and fulfillment
of all the promises of God because
He is the sum and substance of them.

GEOFFREY B. WILSON

Y EARS AGO, WHEN AUTO MANUFACTURERS tried to convince people to buy a certain car, they would try to lure buyers by offering new features and attractive prices. But in recent years, more and more carmakers have tried to win customers by offering longer and more extensive warranties. Today, the competition is so fierce that some companies offer warranties of up to 75,000 or even 100,000 miles!

These warranties really do help sell cars. That's because customers want to protect their expensive investment. They are looking for protection from expensive repair bills and cars that don't live up to their promised performance.

However, every warranty has its limit. No guarantee lasts forever. In fact, at many used car dealerships, dealers refuse to offer any kind of warranty on a car that has over 100,000 miles on it. Why? Because with that much wear and tear, the chances are too great that the car will begin to break down and need expensive repairs. So, after a certain number of years or miles, you are on your own.

> The Lord will come again, and in the coming of the Lord lies the great hope of the believer, his great stimulus to overcome evil, his main incentive to perfect holiness in the fear of the Lord. Oh, to be found blameless in the day of the manifestation of our Lord! God grant us this.
>
> CHARLES SPURGEON

The fact that warranties or guarantees eventually expire is true of just about every man-made gadget available. Computers, appliances, cell phones, watches, and many other such devices are covered for only so long because they wear out. There comes a point where you can no longer hold the manufacturer to his or her original promises about the product.

While that principle is an unfortunate reality here in this physical world, the very opposite is true when it comes to heaven and the spiritual realm. When God makes a promise, it's guaranteed forever. His promises don't change or expire. His track record has always been perfect and will continue to be perfect. So when we see a promise in Scripture, we can be 100 percent absolutely certain it will be fulfilled.

With that in mind, let's read a couple of very exciting and important promises Jesus made to us in John 14:2-3:

> *In My Father's house are many mansions; if it were not so, I would have told you. I go to prepare a place for you. And if I go and prepare a place for you, I will come again and receive you to Myself; that where I am, there you may be also.*

Did you notice the words "if it were not so, I would have told you"? That's another way of saying, "This absolutely *will* happen." We can fully trust what Jesus is telling us. And what does He go on to say?

- He *is* preparing places for us in heaven
- He *will* come again
- He *will* receive us to Himself

There are no *ifs* or *maybes* here. There are no strings attached, no expiration dates. If you are a Christian, you *will* have a home in heaven, and you can be sure Christ *will* come back to take you there. This is Jesus' first mention of the rapture of His church; it's the first time He spoke of taking His believers *up* to His Father's house. In other places in the New Testament Jesus spoke of coming *down* to the earth to set up His kingdom—that's what happens after the second coming. But here Jesus describes the first phase of His coming, or the rapture. And the promise He makes here is a promise you can trust.

Notice also that Jesus said His Father's house has "many mansions." This house is grand indeed! It has enough rooms to accommodate every believer from the Old Testament all the way through the entire church age. Do you question the size of such a house? Don't. It is our Savior's word. Let us dwell in the promise of this great house!

I (Tim) cannot think of this house's glory without remembering my godly mother. Life was hard for her. When she was only 28 years old, she was left a widow with three children. She worked tirelessly in a factory to raise us, attending Bible college at night for nine years and finally receiving her degree so she could become a child evangelism director. She served Christ in this capacity for 23 years. She often lived in one-bedroom apartments or mobile homes. She served in surrender with little emphasis on the material

> Those who have professed faith in Christ will one day be with Him for eternity. He will come for His church and will not forget His promise. Just as Jesus did not forget His promise to the thief on the cross, He will not forget us.
>
> CHARLES STANLEY

things in life. She never owned a home of her own. But heaven will be different. There's a grand house on the way—her real home! She will enjoy this house forever, a house prepared by her Savior.

How encouraging to know this will be our home, too. Its beauty and splendor will be far beyond anything that could be built here on earth. And more importantly, we will be taken there by Jesus Christ Himself. He will take us there because He wants us to dwell together with Him. Doesn't that make you feel pretty special?

*They speak of how you are
looking forward to the coming
of God's Son from heaven…*

1 THESSALONIANS 1:10 NLT

Anticipation or Apathy?

*No man will be anxious for Christ to come
while he has everything he wants here below,
and is quite satisfied with it.... You must set
loose...the world, or you cannot sincerely say to Jesus,
"Come," and that is the very spirit of an earnest worker.*

CHARLES SPURGEON

As a pastor, I (Tim) have had the opportunity to watch many weddings with a clear view of the entire audience. And it's obvious that one of the more emotional and exciting moments of the ceremony is that brief lull just before the bride enters the church or chapel. The groom, his groomsmen, and bridesmaids have all finished marching into the church and are standing on the front platform, awaiting the bride's entrance. The music has stopped momentarily, and the silence seems to magnify the intensity of the moment. Every single eye in the room is riveted on the doorway at the back of the room, waiting for the bride to enter in her glorious splendor. Those few seconds seem unbearably long because everyone is on edge with such great anticipation. At the moment she enters, the enormous tension of anticipation gives way to an instantaneous surge of smiling faces and teary eyes. And the joy of that grand moment continues to linger as she slowly makes her way down the aisle toward her beloved, who has been especially eager for her appearance.

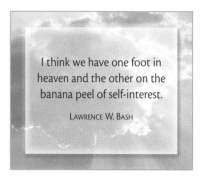

I think we have one foot in heaven and the other on the banana peel of self-interest.

LAWRENCE W. BASH

That's the same kind of anticipation we as Christians ought to have for the return of Christ. We ought to wait longingly for that time when He will come to deliver His own, pour out His righteous judgment upon His wicked foes, and establish His kingdom. In 1 Thessalonians 1:6-10, the apostle Paul tells the Christians in Thessalonica that the Christians in Greece "speak of how you are *looking forward* to the coming of God's Son from heaven" (verse 10 NLT). In other words, it was obvious they were

The object of Christian hope is Christ in His revelation, in His presence, in His communication to us for glory.

ALEXANDER MACLAREN

eager for Christ's return. Their anticipation was so great others couldn't miss it.

Does that describe us as well? Or do we find ourselves forgetting about His future coming...or even hoping that He delays His return?

It's so easy to become attached to the things of this world to the extent that our enthusiasm for Christ's return is diminished. We want to achieve certain personal goals, acquire a certain level of material prosperity, or continue to indulge in various pleasures that aren't necessarily wrong but still distract us from having a heavenly focus in our lives. We find ourselves secretly hoping the Lord won't come back for a while because we don't want our lives interrupted.

Yet Christ's return should be a *welcome* "interruption." Which is more important: My personal goals, or restoring righteousness to this world? My accomplishments, or the establishment of Christ's perfect kingdom? My

The world calls it "wise financial planning" and "attaining our goals" and "the realization of success," but what it really amounts to is *control*. Just about everything most people (including Christians) do in this life is aimed at achieving and maintaining control...so that we do not have to be dependent upon anything or anybody else (including God). But God doesn't want us in control. God wants His people to surrender everything to Him...including our desired control over the affairs and circumstances of our lives.

LARRY SINCLAIR

pleasures, or a true heavenly joy every Christian will experience in Christ's kingdom—a kingdom free from the effects of temptation and sin?

The world as we know it will be completely transformed under Christ's rule. War will be replaced by peace. Selfishness will be replaced by contentment. Hostility will be replaced by kindness. Evil will be replaced by good. Falsehood will be replaced by truth. Despair will be replaced by hope. Hatred will be replaced by love. We can go on and on. The world will be an infinitely better place when Christ comes back. How can we *not* look forward to His return?

> He is the delight of our souls, and He rejoices over us with singing. Rejoice that He has chosen you and called you, and through the betrothal look forward to the marriage.
>
> CHARLES SPURGEON

Don't let the momentary things of this world rob you of the joyful anticipation of Christ's return. Keep your eyes focused heavenward. We have a great future to look forward to. And yes, the wait will be longer than the brief wait that takes place before a bride's entrance at a wedding ceremony. Our wait could be much longer. But it will be very much worthwhile, because all the spiritual riches God bestows upon us at that time will last for eternity.

Be ready, for the Son of Man is coming at an hour when you do not expect Him. Who then is a faithful and wise servant, whom his master made ruler over his household, to give them food in due season? Blessed is that servant whom his master, when he comes, will find so doing.

MATTHEW 24:44-46

A READINESS THAT
LEADS TO ACTION

*The imminent return of our Lord is
the great Bible argument for a pure, unselfish,
devoted, unworldly, active life of service.*

R. A. TORREY

WHEN IT COMES TO CHRIST'S RETURN, there are two kinds of
Christians: those who wait passively, and those who wait
actively.

When I say certain Christians wait passively, I mean
that the knowledge of Christ's return does not have an
impact on how they live. By contrast, those who wait
actively are ever aware that Christ could come at any
time, and it's made evident by their actions.

Jesus Himself pointed this out during His last week on
earth. In Matthew 24:45-51 He tells a parable that contrasts
a faithful servant with an unfaithful one. He describes the

wise servant as one who continues to work hard even while his master is gone on a trip. By contrast, the foolish servant slacks off while the master is away. Yet he's caught by surprise when the master returns unexpectedly—and he's punished for his unfaithfulness. That's why it's so important for us to heed Jesus' warning stated at the beginning of the parable: "Be ready, for the Son of Man is coming at an hour when you do not expect Him" (verse 44).

> The Spirit of Christ is the spirit of missions, and the nearer we get to Him the more intensely missionary we become.
>
> HENRY MARTYN

I (Tim) once saw the faithful servant's diligence graphically illustrated in the lives of a young dentist and his wife. They accepted Christ in our church many years ago. Later, this couple joined the Campus Crusade for Christ staff and served in the Churches Alive program. They spent the next 30 years teaching thousands of people how to share their faith in Christ. Recently they began to read our Left Behind series and wrote to tell us how much they enjoyed the books. In the same letter, they reminded me that shortly after their conversion I had been teaching the book of Revelation on Sunday nights. The man freely admitted, "In those days, I must confess, I didn't always understand what you were teaching even when my wife tried to explain it to me as we drove home from church.

But one thing I did learn was that Jesus was coming, and I had better get my house in order!"

Putting their house in order, of course, simply meant being available to serve the Lord. Like the Thessalonians we read about in the previous chapter, this couple put into action their anticipation of Christ's return. Their enthusiasm for the soon

> As we earnestly seek God for revival, we must not forsake the essential tasks of the church; preaching the truth, evangelism, and a vital interest in and support for missions.
>
> ERROLL HULSE

return of Christ led to a concern for doing whatever they could to make sure other people could come to salvation before it was too late. Looking back, the dentist was able to say in his letter, "It's been a great life." And because he and his wife were active in doing the Master's work, they won't be caught by surprise when the Master returns.

All through the years of my ministry I have never heard anyone complain that they had made a wrong decision in surrendering their lives to Christ. The reason is simple: The committed Christian life is the only meaningful way to live. And at the center of that meaning is the glorious hope of our Lord's return.

> We need to hold the present with a slack hand, so as to be ready to fold our tents and take to the road if God will.
>
> ALEXANDER MACLAREN

*W*hen He had spoken these things,
while they watched, He was taken up,
and a cloud received Him out of their
sight. And while they looked steadfastly
toward heaven as He went up, behold,
two men stood by them in white
apparel, who also said, "Men of Galilee,
why do you stand gazing up into
heaven? This same Jesus, who was
taken up from you into heaven,
will so come in like manner as you
saw Him go into heaven."

ACTS 1:9-11

HE WILL RETURN!

And Lord, haste the day when the faith shall be sight,
The clouds be rolled back as a scroll,
The trump shall resound and the Lord shall descend,
Even so, it is well with my soul.

HORATIO G. SPAFFORD

When ANGELS SPEAK, THEY SPEAK FOR GOD. They speak for all time. And while the disciples watched in dismay as Christ left their midst and ascended into heaven, it was the angels who said, "This same Jesus, who was taken up from you into heaven, will so come in like manner as you saw Him go into heaven" (Acts 1:11).

Jesus will return the same way He left. At His second coming, He will descend both physically and visibly. In the same way that many people saw Him go up in the clouds, many will see Him come down in the clouds. Jesus said that when He comes back, the whole world will take notice: "Then all the tribes of the earth will mourn, and they will see the Son of Man coming on the clouds of heaven with power and great glory" (Matthew 24:30). It's going to be impossible for anyone to miss this climactic event!

Yet there are some who say, "Jesus left 2000 years ago and He still hasn't come back." They're like the scoffers in 2 Peter 3:4 who say, "Where is the promise of His coming?" If it hasn't happened yet, they reason, it just isn't going to happen. Then there are those who say that Jesus' return would be spiritual and not physical.

No mind is much employed upon the present; recollection and anticipation fill up almost all our moments.

SAMUEL JOHNSON

But the promise of Christ's physical return to earth is proclaimed loudly and clearly all through the Bible. This isn't some small, obscure statement buried deep in a Scripture passage that's difficult to interpret. The angels couldn't have been any clearer when they said, "This same Jesus, who was taken up from you into heaven, will so come in like manner as you saw Him go into heaven." Christ Himself couldn't have been any clearer when He said, "They will see the Son of Man coming on the clouds of heaven with power and great glory." The apostle Paul couldn't have been any clearer when he said, "We should live soberly, righteously, and godly in the present age, looking for the blessed hope and glorious appearing of our great God and Savior Jesus Christ."

If the angels, Jesus, and Paul were wrong, then God's Word cannot be trusted. If Jesus isn't going to come back, then we have a God who cannot keep His promises. If He can't ensure to us that Christ will return, then how can we trust Him to guarantee our salvation, meet our needs here on earth, and take us home to heaven? The fact is, God has fulfilled hundreds of promises already, and He will fulfill all the rest. Though 2000 years have gone by since Jesus ascended into the clouds, we do not need to begin worrying about the possibility He won't come back.

> The millennial kingdom will provide our Lord and Savior, the Messiah Jesus Christ, with an opportunity to reign over a world that will be as it was meant to be. Satan will be bound and unable to exercise his influence over God's creation. The blood of the martyrs will have been avenged, and the saints will be joined with our Savior, in a preview of Heaven to come.
>
> BEN RAST

The day is coming when Christ will appear—there's no question about it. And before He does, He will rapture His church and take her to His Father's house. There, we who believe will be judged and given our rewards. In the meantime, the seven-year Tribulation will take place on the earth, during which God will pour out His wrath upon those who reject Him. At the end of that period, Jesus will come with power and glory to the earth to set up His millennial kingdom, and we will return with Him.

Some people have difficulty understanding the fact that the rapture will take place before the Tribulation, and Jesus' second coming will occur afterward. Here's a good way to illustrate what will happen:

In November, when Beverly and I go to the mall, we cannot help but notice all the Christmas decorations everywhere. During one such trip she said, "It looks like Christmas is coming," to which I replied, "Yes, but first we must have Thanksgiving." As Thanksgiving precedes Christmas, so the rapture comes before Christ's visible return to earth.

Here's another illustration: Dietrich Bonhoeffer, a Lutheran pastor in Germany during the Hitler regime, was imprisoned for being one of the few outspoken Christian voices against Hitler's inhumane policies. While in prison, this brilliant theologian wrote several books that will remain a blessing for all time. Tragically, just several days before U.S. troops liberated the people in his camp, he was executed. One of the few creature comforts he was afforded during the long months of his imprisonment was an occasional visit from his fiancée, whom he loved deeply. During one of her visits he asked her not to come to see him too suddenly or unannounced. His anticipation of her coming was nearly as meaningful as her arrival. It gave him so much to look forward to.

So it is with the coming of Jesus. Anticipating each day as though this were the day our Lord returns ought to have a motivating effect on our lives. May the Lord hasten that day!

You yourselves know perfectly
that the day of the Lord
so comes as a thief in the night…
We are not of the night nor
of darkness. Therefore let us
not sleep, as others do, but let us
watch and be sober.

1 Thessalonians 3:12-13

HOW THEN SHOULD WE LIVE?

The certainty of the second coming of Christ should touch and tincture every part of our daily behavior.

JOHN BLANCHARD

WE'VE ALL EXPERIENCED THE TERRIBLE embarrassment that comes when a guest unexpectedly shows up on our doorstep and our house is in disarray. The kids have left their toys all over the floor, there's a basket of dirty laundry sitting in the living room, there are unwashed dishes on the kitchen counter, and you yourself haven't had a chance to make yourself look presentable.

Whatever the case, as soon as you open the door, you offer profuse apologies for the disorderly appearance of your house. And in your mind you're thinking, *Why did you have to stop by right now, of all times? Why didn't you call first and ask if it's okay to come visit?*

> Most meaningful things in life require preparation. We all know the feeling of being prepared as opposed to being unprepared.
>
> BILLY COLEMAN

The possibility of an unexpected visitor is a very good reason for us to keep our house in order at all times. When we make the time and effort to always be ready, we no longer have to worry about being caught off guard. We can relax and enjoy our time with our visitor.

Not only should our physical house be ready at all times, but our spiritual house should be as well. The Bible clearly says that the time of Christ's return will come "as a thief in the night." That's another way of saying it will happen when we least expect it.

> Clearly, then, much mystery clouds our full understanding of many of the features of our Lord's return...Repeatedly in Scripture we are urged to discern the signs of the times, to be watchful, and to be ready.
>
> JOHN MACARTHUR

When a thief wants to rob a house, he doesn't call in advance to say he's stopping by. He comes unannounced, totally by surprise. There's no warning.

The same is true of the rapture and Christ's second coming. We don't know when He's coming back. For that reason, we should always be ready. As the apostle Paul says in 1 Thessalonians 5:6,

"Therefore let us not sleep, as others do, but let us watch and be sober." If you think it's embarrassing to be caught with our physical house in disorder, it's going to be much more so if Christ comes when our spiritual house is all messy.

How can we make sure we're ready? Right after Paul says Christ's coming will be as a thief in the night, he goes on to challenge us to live in constant awareness of that fact:

1. We are to encourage and comfort each other with the promise of hope (1 Thessalonians 5:11).

2. We are to build up each other (verse 12).

3. We are to think highly of and honor those who are our spiritual leaders and teachers (verses 12-13).

4. We are to live peacefully with one another (verse 13).

5. We are to be patient with others, including those who are unruly or weak. One of the hallmarks of the Christian life is that we should be more concerned about others than about ourselves (verse 14).

6. We are to always pursue what is good both for ourselves and others, and not do evil to others (verse 15).

7. We are to rejoice always (verse 16).

8. We are to pray without ceasing—our ongoing communication with God enables us to live with greater spiritual sensitivity (verse 17).

9. We are to always be thankful. Thankful people are joyful people. Rejoicing and thanking go hand in hand. Taken together, they dissolve discouragement and depression.

10. We are to avoid quenching or disappointing the Spirit by harboring sin within us (verse 19).

11. We should not despise prophecies (verse 20). Prophecy should be one of our delights (see Revelation 19:10).

12. We are to "test all things; hold fast what is good" (verse 21).

13. We are to "abstain from every form of evil" (verse 22).

All through that list, we see two constant themes: 1) living in harmony with fellow believers, and 2) living rightly in our relationship with God. When these are in place, we're not going to be caught red-faced with embarrassment when Christ comes to rapture us.

Is your spiritual house ready? Are you living in anticipation of the most important guest in your life? There's nothing like the total peace that comes with living in constant readiness. It's a peace that will set your heart and mind at rest, and a peace that will free you to truly enjoy your relationships with God and other believers.

> A good day ending with profound inner peace is a day in which we have fought the good fight, run the race, and kept the faith.
>
> DR. LLOYD JOHN OGILVIE

Our present troubles are quite small and won't last very long. Yet they produce for us an immeasurably great glory that will last forever! So, we don't look at the troubles we can see right now; rather, we look forward to what we have not yet seen. For the troubles we see will soon be over, but the joys to come will last forever.

2 Corinthians 4:17-18 nlt

NEVER
GIVE UP

*One thought of eternity makes
all earthly sorrows fade away.*

BASILEA SCHLINK

DISCOURAGEMENT IS ONE OF THE PRINCIPAL TOOLS Satan uses to defeat Christians. If we allow him to somehow take our eyes off Jesus and His coming, Satan can render us useless to God. He knows that through discouragement, he can get us to focus downward and inward upon our problems in self-pity. And when we're absorbed with ourselves, it's very difficult for us to serve Christ and others.

In 2 Corinthians 4:17-18, Paul exhorts us not to give up. He says, "Our present troubles are quite small and won't last very long" (NLT). Now, when you're right in the middle of difficult circumstances or painful suffering, it's hard to believe that your troubles are small. The dark and ominous clouds of our problems have a way of blotting out any sunshine in our lives. And when there's no sunshine in sight, it's challenging to remain optimistic or hopeful.

At times like that, it's helpful for us to imagine placing our trial, our suffering, our pain on a timeline that stretches from our birth all the way into eternity. What happens? It becomes small in comparison to the whole of our life, and especially in comparison to all eternity. What's more, we can rest assured that every single one of our problems will disappear completely at death. They won't follow us into eternity. After we've been in heaven for 10,000 years, the troubles that plagued us during our 80 or so years of life on earth will seem microscopic indeed.

With that in mind, we need to remember not to let the temporary cares and afflictions of this life become magnified out of proportion. We must not allow them to dominate our thinking, or they will cause us to lose heart.

Then there's the whole matter of what we feed into our minds. Have you noticed how watching the news or reading the paper can build an odd negativity into life? Probably one of the worst things we can do is to watch the news just before going to bed, or letting our minds dwell on our personal worries or frustrations. This leads us to go to bed with a negative mind-set, and may end up causing us to become discouraged or to exaggerate any anxieties that are already in our lives.

How much better it would be for us to nurture our minds with positive input. In Philippians 4:8, Paul tells us, "Whatever things are true, whatever things are noble, whatever things are just, whatever things are pure, whatever things are lovely, whatever things are of good report, if there is any virtue and if there is anything praiseworthy—meditate

This world is our passage, not our portion.

MATTHEW HENRY

on these things." The word "meditate" means "to focus one's thoughts on," or "to ponder." Can you imagine the positive effect of reading God's wonderful promises in the Bible at bedtime? Especially the promises related to the rapture, the second coming, and eternity. It's these kinds of thoughts that lift us up and encourage us. They help us to remember that our trials are only temporary, and the joy we'll experience in heaven will last forever and ever.

My family and I (Tim) have been lifetime football fans. For a while I had the privilege of teaching a Bible study for the San Diego Chargers. In one game against Kansas City, the Chargers had been behind for the entire game. John Hadel was the quarterback and Lance Allworth was his wide receiver. It was a high-scoring game, and toward the end, the Chargers were down by three points. On the very last play, with just two seconds to go, John threw a long pass into the end zone and Lance leaped four feet into the air to catch it. He made the touchdown, and the Chargers won.

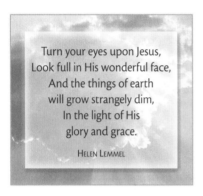

Turn your eyes upon Jesus,
Look full in His wonderful face,
And the things of earth
will grow strangely dim,
In the light of His
glory and grace.

HELEN LEMMEL

I have often compared the second coming of Jesus to that football game. Historically, Christians have seemed defeated during the 2000 years that have elapsed since our Lord ascended to heaven. Believers have suffered persecution, ridicule, rejection, martyrdom, and even crucifixion. It sometimes looks as though we will never catch up and win the game. But don't lose heart; keep looking to Jesus. He is coming, and we will win!

*Of that day and hour
no one knows, no, not even
the angels of heaven, nor the Son,
but the Father alone.*

A GREAT
MYSTERY

Christ hath told us He will come,
but not when, that we might never put off
our clothes, or put out the candle.

WILLIAM GURNALL

THERE'S ONE VERY BIG MYSTERY IN THE BIBLE that some Christians have a hard time with—the timing of Christ's return. Scripture is overwhelmingly clear about the fact that no one knows when this will happen. Yet you would be amazed at how many Christians have a hard time accepting that. Whenever Jerry and I travel to different cities to promote the Left Behind series, we always meet people who come up to us and ask, "So when do you think the Lord will return?" They want to know exactly when Jesus will return, and they are persistent in the hopes of finding clues that will give them the answer.

In fact, some Christians express downright disappointment that God hasn't revealed this information. And then there are those who are convinced that the answer is secretly hidden in the Bible and that if we hit upon the right formula, we can decode the mystery and figure out the date of the rapture or the second coming or both.

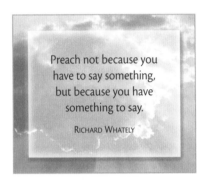

Preach not because you have to say something, but because you have something to say.

RICHARD WHATELY

But neither of those responses is healthy. In fact, they're harmful. Can you imagine what could easily happen if we as Christians *did* know the timing of Christ's return? We would probably be just like the students who delay studying for a test or put off writing a term paper until the last minute. We would feel little urgency about living a holy life or leading other people to Christ until just a short time before the Lord's return.

What's more, non-Christians would probably say, "Why become a Christian now? There's no hurry. Time is on my side. I'll make a decision for Christ just before He comes." Such people aren't really interested in following God. They want to get away with doing their own thing for as long as they can, then try to get into heaven in the nick of time.

So, there are definite benefits to not knowing when Jesus will return. It keeps us on our toes. It compels us to live wisely, "redeeming the time, because the days are evil" (Ephesians 5:16). It teaches us that holy living at all times is important so that we might attract lost souls to Christ. It teaches us the urgency of evangelism and missions, for we don't know how much time is left for the lost people of this world.

One Sunday evening in 1871, the great evangelist Dwight L. Moody preached to a large audience of listeners in Chicago, sharing with them about Christ and the way of salvation. At the end of his message, he encouraged the people to think about what he had said and to come back the next Sunday night with their hearts ready to receive Christ.

Well, for many of the people in that crowd, next Sunday night never came. At the same time Moody concluded the meeting, the city fire bells sounded. Chicago was rapidly engulfed by enormous and fast-moving flames

> Now is the time to prepare for that day. Instead of living in submission to the dictates of a world and society that is soon to be judged by our righteous God, live as more than a conqueror through Him who loves you and gave Himself for you.
>
> KAY ARTHUR

that destroyed many thousands of buildings, took more than a thousand lives, and left more than 100,000 people homeless. Moody's church and home were wiped out as well. But those losses had no effect on him because his worldly possessions meant nothing to him. Rather, his heart grieved bitterly over the people who, because of the fire, had lost their lives and would not be coming back the next week to make Christ their Savior and receive eternal life.

As a result, Moody promised he would never again preach without urging people to receive Christ right then and there. We can never assume that there will be a tomorrow, that there will be another chance. Every day counts, every moment matters. When we live with that perspective, then we will never have any regrets about lost opportunities.

*God did not appoint us
to wrath, but to obtain
salvation through
our Lord Jesus Christ....*

1 Thessalonians 5:9

Saved from the Wrath to Come

If we are believers in Jesus Christ we have already come through the storm of judgment. It happened at the cross.

Billy Graham

The promise found in 1 Thessalonians 5:9—that "God did not appoint us to wrath, but to obtain salvation through our Lord Jesus Christ"—is one of the most underappreciated promises in the Bible.

The "wrath" mentioned in this verse refers to the great outpouring of God's judgment during the Tribulation. How do we know? By the context in which the verse appears. The apostle Paul begins this chapter of the Bible by talking about Christ's return, which will come "as a thief in the night" (verse 2). And all the way to verse 9, where we read that we're not appointed to wrath, Paul gives instructions for how to live in the days preceding the Lord's return.

If you've read our Left Behind series, then you know that in the first book, millions of Christians instantaneously disappear from the face of the earth. They are raptured to heaven. After that comes the Tribulation—the seven years of horrible judgments God unleashes on those who have not yet repented of their sinful ways. During those seven years, many millions of people will become Christians—there will be a massive soul harvest. But those of us who are believers *before* the Tribulation will not go through it. Instead, we will be spared from this time of judgment because we're not appointed to wrath.

Tragically, there is a small but growing number of people who say Christians will go through this period of horrible judgment upon the earth. They say the rapture won't happen until during the Tribulation or at the end of it. That's a pretty frightening perspective, isn't it? Again, if you've read our Left Behind series, you have some idea of just how horrible those days will be. Christians will be persecuted as never before, with literally millions of martyrs.

Is that what we're destined for? The Bible doesn't seem to say so. Not only does 1 Thessalonians 5:9 say we're not appointed to wrath, but 1 Thessalonians 1:10 says that Jesus will deliver us "from the wrath to come." And in Revelation 3:10, Jesus Himself says, "I also will keep you from the hour of trial which shall come upon the whole world." Because Jesus made this statement in a letter written to the church in the ancient city of Philadelphia, some say He was referring to a persecution that would affect the Christians in that city in their immediate future. But the passage speaks of an "hour of trial" that will be experienced by "the *whole* world." The historical record clearly indicates that didn't happen back then, which means it must be a still-future event.

> Are you ready? Are you ready?
> Ready for the Judgment Day?
> When the saints and the sinners
> Shall be parted right and left—
> Are you ready for
> the Judgment Day?
>
> METHODIST HYMN

Notice also that in Revelation chapters 4 through 19, where we read a detailed overview of the Tribulation, we find absolutely no mention of the church. Why? Because it's no longer on the earth! The church will have been raptured into heaven by Jesus Christ.

Finally, we have to consider the purpose of the Tribulation. It's a time of judgment—and God's judgment is reserved for the wicked who refuse to turn from their sin. Those of us who are Christians don't need to face God's judgment; Jesus already took care of that at the cross. That's why Romans 8:1 says, "There is therefore now no condemnation to those who are in Christ Jesus."

Indeed, God promises to spare us from the horrors of the Tribulation. He did not appoint us to wrath. Instead, He has appointed for Jesus to prepare a place for us in heaven, and for Jesus to come receive us and take us to that place. There, we will be safe in His all-protecting hands. Ours is a future not of trepidation and fear, but of confidence and hope.

Vengeance is Mine, I will repay,"
says the Lord.

Romans 12:19

GOD'S JUSTICE
WILL PREVAIL

*Now Christianity teaches us how to behave
toward our enemies; and in this instruction
it quite differs from all other rules and methods....
Whoever are our enemies, that wish us ill
and seek to do us ill, our rule is to do
them no hurt, but all the good we can.*

MATTHEW HENRY

HAVE YOU EVER GOTTEN ANGRY AT HOW some people frequently seem to get away with their wicked behavior? When you see a reckless driver on the highway, you've probably found yourself wishing that a police officer were around to catch them. Or consider the newspaper articles you've read about terrible crimes that cannot be traced to their perpetrators, who end up going unpunished. You want so badly to see justice done, and you become frustrated when that doesn't happen.

More pointedly, you can probably remember times when someone provoked or hurt you and you wanted to strike back. You wanted to get even—perhaps not physically, but verbally or some other way. How often have you rehearsed in your mind the things you wanted to say to an enemy, only to later realize that revenge is not the answer?

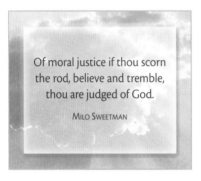

Of moral justice if thou scorn the rod, believe and tremble, thou are judged of God.

MILO SWEETMAN

We've all been through that. Or, perhaps you did take vengeance…and then you felt guilty afterward. If so, that's because God tells us, "Repay no one evil for evil" and, "If it is possible, as much as depends on you, live peaceably with all men" (Romans 12:17-18). When we violate those spiritual principles, the Holy Spirit will convict us of our error.

When it comes to justice, God assures us that the guilty won't get away. He has promised, "Vengeance is Mine, I will repay" (Romans 12:19). That's a powerful statement with no hint of uncertainly whatsoever. God will mete out judgment to those who deserve it. He will punish those who have done wrong. Nothing escapes His eyes; He is all-knowing. Because He has perfect wisdom, perfect knowledge, and is perfectly righteous, He will give out perfectly just sentences. We humans, by contrast, cannot see the hearts of other people or understand their motives. That's why it's so much better that we leave vengeance in God's hands.

God's promise to judge the wicked will be fulfilled in a number of ways. One of the more significant expressions of His judgment will take place during the Tribulation, and the most important one is the future Great White Throne judgment, at which the unbelievers of all the ages will be sent to their final eternal destination and punishment.

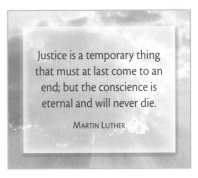

Justice is a temporary thing that must at last come to an end; but the conscience is eternal and will never die.

MARTIN LUTHER

While we may relish the satisfaction of knowing that the wicked will receive what's due to them, God has not called us to take delight in that fact. Rather, look at what He says in the Bible:

- "If your enemy hungers, feed him; if he thirsts, give him a drink....Do not be overcome by evil, but overcome evil with good" (Romans 12:20-21).

- "I say to you, love your enemies, bless those who curse you, do good to those who hate you, and pray for those who spitefully use you and persecute you" (Matthew 5:44).

When someone wrongs us, our immediate reaction is to strike back. But God has called us to do the complete opposite! We're to love and pray for those who mean harm to us. The world teaches us to get even, but God teaches us to show kindness. That's tough to do, isn't it? Why do you suppose God asks us to repay evil with good?

As long as we're on this earth, our lives can shine forth to a lost world that's desperately in need of God's love and

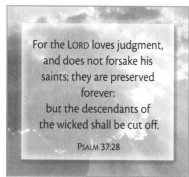

For the LORD loves judgment, and does not forsake his saints; they are preserved forever: but the descendants of the wicked shall be cut off.

PSALM 37:28

forgiveness. It's when people see God's love in us that they're more likely to be attracted to Him—much like a moth in the dark night is attracted to light. God's heart grieves for those who are unsaved—He is "not willing that any should perish but that all should come to repentance" (2 Peter 3:9). As long as Christ hasn't returned yet, there's time for unbelievers to receive Christ as their Savior.

Loving and praying for our enemies may not come easy to us. But with God, all things are possible. He has promised to enable us, and we need only to yield ourselves to that enablement. When that happens, we make ourselves a light God can use to win people to Christ.

*The fire will test each one's work,
of what sort it is. If anyone's work
which he has built on it endures,
he will receive a reward.*

1 CORINTHIANS 3:13-14

Rewards for the Faithful

The gospel teaches us that while believers are not rewarded on account of their works, they are rewarded according to their works.

R. L. Dabney

THERE'S THE STORY OF A POPULAR and successful home-builder who was so good at his craft that he had a long waiting list of people who wanted homes built for them. This builder was a true artisan who was meticulous about his work. The houses he built were beautiful and, more importantly, well-constructed.

Through the years, this man's son occasionally tagged along with dad and helped out on the construction site by doing odd jobs. When he was little, he would sweep up the sawdust and pick up stray nails on the ground. As the boy became older, the father entrusted him with more responsibilities. He trained his son in the proper use of equipment and the secrets of good craftsmanship. The father was very exacting in all he did and expected the son to be likewise.

When the son finished school and was ready to enter the work world, the father hired him as a junior partner. One day he told his son, "I have an important project for you, and I'm going to put you in charge of it. The site is on top of a hill and has a breathtaking view. The home is bigger than any you've worked on before and should be built with the greatest of care and the best materials. Here are the blueprints. The future owner has high expectations, and I feel confident you're ready to handle this job on your own."

The son, with great enthusiasm, poured a great amount of time and energy into building the home. He went the extra mile in every possible way, making sure this home was the very best it could possibly be. He wanted the future owner to be pleased—he did not want to risk causing any disappointment that would reflect badly on his father's reputation as a homebuilder.

At long last, the project was completed. The home sparkled—the son had done an outstanding job. When the father came by to inspect the home, tears filled his eyes. "I'm proud of you, son," he said. "You did a great job. This home is going to be very special to your mother and me because it was built with your hands."

The son didn't know what to say. On the one hand, he was filled with pride at his hard work. But on the other, he felt as if he had been deceived by his father. He had envisioned perhaps a wealthy or famous person in town becoming the owner of the house. Instead, the home was for his parents. Sad to say, he felt resentment in his heart, but didn't say anything.

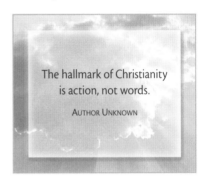

The hallmark of Christianity is action, not words.

AUTHOR UNKNOWN

A couple of weeks later, the father approached his son again. "I have an even bigger project for you. It's for a large home on a beautiful lakefront property. In fact, it's even more magnificent than the one you just built. Because you did such a great job, I decided to give you full charge of this project as well."

The son willingly took the assignment...but he was still angry toward his father. Looking at the blueprints, he could see his father was right. This home would truly be grand. The plans even called for a massive outdoor deck and a dock that extended out over the lake.

This time, however, the son didn't put his heart into his work. He did everything he could to cut corners, reduce expenses, and save time. Instead of getting the best raw materials, he got discounted or slightly damaged goods. Instead of exacting work, he became slipshod. And the money he saved wasn't deducted from the future owner's bill. Instead, it went into his own pocket. When the home was completed, the exterior trimmings were applied with just enough care to hide the flaws within.

As was his custom, the father came by for an inspection. Unaware of the poor craftsmanship cleverly hidden under the fresh paint and exterior trimmings, the father beamed his approval and patted his son on the back. "I'm so proud that you're following in my footsteps. In fact, I bet you'll become an even better builder than your dad. Beginning today, I want you to take over my business." Then he paused. "And, by the way, this is now your home, son. Here are the keys."

Can you imagine how the son felt this time? From all external appearances, the house appeared to be a jewel. But the son knew the truth. And now, the home was his. Instant regret seared his heart. Now he realized how foolish he had been.

All of us who are Christians are workers—workers for God. He has entrusted us with certain responsibilities. In His church, there are some of us who teach, some of us who help organize activities, and some of us who serve by doing seemingly insignificant things, such as tying children's shoestrings and giving them a cup of milk and cookies. But no matter what you do, if it's done for the Lord, it's *extremely* significant. If it's done for Him, it's important.

Are we doing our service to the very best of our ability? Are we putting forth our best effort? By the way, our service to God happens not only at church, but in our homes and workplaces as well. How is our service to God as a father, a mother, a husband, a wife, a friend, a coworker?

Someday, God will test our works. "We are God's fellow workers....If any man builds on this foundation using gold, silver, costly stones, wood, hay, or straw, his work will be shown for what it is, because the Day will bring it to light. It will be revealed with fire, and the fire will test the quality of each man's work. If what he has built survives, he will receive his reward. If it is burned up, he will suffer loss; he himself will be saved, but only as one escaping through the flames" (1 Corinthians 3:9,12-15).

Are you building with gold, silver, costly stones? They will survive the fire, and you will be rewarded by God. Or are you building with wood, hay, and straw? These materials won't last; they won't survive God's test. As a Christian, you won't lose your salvation. You'll still go to heaven. But your work won't be worthy of reward. And remember—while the son was

> This is sacred service, this is God's work: praying, communing, preaching, buying, selling, bricklaying, doing whatsoever things providence has thrust into your hand to do—doing them for glory.
>
> WAYLAND HOYT

able to hide his slipshod construction work from his father, we won't be able to hide anything from our heavenly Father. He knows our ulterior motives and our heart.

Whatever we do for God, then, may it be done in the very best way possible!

*W*e must all appear before
the judgment seat of Christ, that
each one may receive the things done in
the body, according to what he has
done, whether good or bad. Knowing,
therefore, the terror of the Lord,
we persuade men…For if we are
beside ourselves, it is for God…For
the love of Christ constrains us.

2 CORINTHIANS 5:10-11,13-14

A PROMISE THAT
CALLS FOR COMPASSION

*Only a burdened heart can
lead to fruitful service.*

ALAN REDPATH

THE APOSTLE PAUL MUST HAVE BEEN ONE OF the most motivated—and compassionate—Christians in the first century. Not only did he travel far and wide to help start
numerous churches, but he also cared deeply for both the
nurture of Christians and the winning of unbelievers to
Christ.

What motivated Paul? Many things did, but three moti-
vators stand out in particular, and all three are found in
the Scripture passage at the beginning of this devotion. All
three also reveal the tremendous compassion he had for

other people—a compassion that ought to mark our own lives as well.

The first motivator of the apostle was the fact that "we must all appear before the judgment seat of Christ" (2 Corinthians 5:10). We who are Christians will face this judgment when Jesus comes to rapture His church. Our appearance at this heavenly court is not related to our salvation; that matter was already settled by our Savior at the cross. Rather, this judgment has to do with our works. It will be an evaluation of whether our works were done out of good motives or selfish ones, and we will be rewarded for those things that were done out of a pure heart and true diligence.

> Be not therefore high-minded, but fear. Rejoice, but let it be with trembling. As the elect of God, put on, not only humbleness of mind, but bowels of compassion; and pray, O pray for your unconverted brethren!
>
> George Whitefield

The second motivator was the love of Christ (verse 14—"the love of Christ constrains [or drives] us"). Who can read the account of Paul's service in Acts chapters 13 through 28 and fail to notice his great love for the One who saved him on the Damascus Road? Paul suffered unbelievable hardships during his years of ministry...all because he loved Christ so much. Remember when Paul was stoned by his enemies and left for dead at Lystra? Even after that frightening experience, the love of Christ motivated him to get up and walk to the next city to preach. Persecution and the threat of death didn't scare him away or diminish his love for serving Christ.

Third, Paul was motivated by the horrible judgment that awaits unbelievers. He said, "Knowing, therefore, the terror of the Lord, we persuade men" (verse 11). God is a just and righteous God, and He will not let sin go unpunished. Knowing that, we ought to beseech people to receive Christ as their Savior.

Unfortunately, too many of us are afraid to talk about sin candidly with others. We fear that if we warn people of future judgment, we'll scare them away. Instead, we concentrate on the love and mercy of God, giving some people the impression that God is but a doting old grandfather who is willing to overlook our carnality and indifference. Not so! The same Bible that teaches the love of God teaches His justice as well. And Jesus Himself repeatedly warned people to repent of their sins lest they face eternal condemnation. Jesus, the most merciful person who ever lived on this earth, was merciful to the point of being completely honest about the consequences of remaining unrepentant.

Paul had a correct perspective of God's justice and righteousness. He lived in a healthy and reverential fear that he might drop his cup of responsibility and disappoint his Father in heaven. Knowing the "terror of the

Lord" and the reality of future judgment, he persuaded men to become saved. A few verses later, in 1 Corinthians 5:20, he said, "We are ambassadors for Christ, as though God were pleading through us: we implore you on Christ's behalf, be reconciled to God."

This call to persuasion is our business, too. As ambassadors of Christ, we are to share our faith with others and urge them to "be reconciled to God." The Bible's warnings about the certainty of future judgment ought to compel our hearts to express compassion to those who are destined for eternal punishment.

> From that moment in which the blessings of the Cross become my own, my life is committed to the publication of the evangel of the Cross to all men; from that moment in which the compassion of God becomes my salvation, I am called on to live in the power of that compassion for the salvation of others.
>
> G. CAMPBELL MORGAN

And, like the ambassadors of any foreign power, our message is not our own and may be rejected. Still, our responsibility is to convey the message... regardless of how it is received. When people ridicule us for our faith, we need to remember not to take it personally. Jesus said, "If the world hates you, you know that it hated Me before it hated you" (John 15:18).

May we have the same compassion as the apostle Paul and serve as ambassadors who are motivated by the fact that Jesus is coming soon. May our hearts yearn to introduce other people into Christ's kingdom.

For as the lightning comes from the east and flashes to the west, so also will the coming of the Son of Man be…Then the sign of the Son of Man will appear in heaven, and then all the tribes of the earth will mourn, and they will see the Son of Man coming on the clouds of heaven with power and great glory.

MATTHEW 24:27,30

In Power and
Great Glory

*He who came in humility and shame
will return in spectacular magnificence.*

John R. W. Stott

Quite a stir was raised some 20 years ago when, without
warning, a prominent full-page ad appeared in the *Los
Angeles Times* and proclaimed that Christ had returned
and His identity would soon be revealed to the inhabitants
of earth. Nothing in the ad indicated its origin, which
made it hard for anyone to investigate the claims. Instead,
people were told that this "Christ" would soon make
Himself known.

The ad elicited an interesting variety of responses.
Some Christians got nervous and wondered if somehow
they had missed out on the Lord's second coming. Others

raised their eyebrows in skepticism, noting that the statements in the ad strongly contradicted the Bible's teachings on the Lord's return. Some unbelievers wanted to know if this meant judgment was coming soon. And others shrugged their shoulders in disdain, chalking this up as just another wacky prediction from some religious fanatics.

While many people couldn't agree on what the ad meant, one thing was certain: It got a lot of people thinking. Most surprising of all was the number of Christians who wondered if the ad should be taken seriously. Had Christ really come back? Were we entering or already in the last days?

> Lo, He comes with clouds descending,
> Once for favored sinners slain;
> Thousand thousand saints attending
> Swell the triumph of His train:
> Alleluia, alleluia!
> God appears on earth to reign.
>
> CHARLES WESLEY

The reason we say this was surprising is that, according to the Bible, when Christ returns, people won't need a newspaper advertisement to tell them about it. Scripture says the second coming will be so obvious people won't miss it. Matthew 24:27 says Jesus will come as the lightning comes from the east and flashes to the west—which means He will come suddenly. Verse 30 adds, "The sign of the Son of Man will appear in heaven, and *all* the tribes of the earth will mourn, and they will *see* the Son of Man coming on the clouds of heaven with power and great glory." *All* the people of the earth will see this event!

Christ won't be hidden in some special location and then call a press conference to proclaim His arrival. No, He will burst forth from heaven "with power and great glory"! That's what God promised, and that's exactly how it will happen.

Sad to say, there are many people who have been deluded by misunderstandings about

> God has a plan and a purpose, and He is the One who knows what will happen, not only tomorrow, but also years from now. He knows the moment of His Son's return to earth and all that will take place before His Second Coming.
>
> CHARLES STANLEY

Christ's second coming. Jehovah's Witnesses, for instance, teach that Jesus returned invisibly in 1914 and is spiritually present with us. Then there are certain Christians known as preterists who teach that Jesus' return, as described in Matthew 24:27-30, took place in A.D. 70. If that's true, then the whole world missed out on this important event, for no historians or early Christians left any record of such taking place.

It helps us to remember what Jesus said in Matthew 24:23-24: "If anyone says to you, 'Look, here is the Christ!' or 'There!' do not believe it. For false christs and false prophets will arise and show great signs and wonders, so as to deceive, if possible, even the elect." When Jesus returns, it'll be very obvious what's happening. No one will have to explain what's going on. And a newspaper advertisement won't be needed to call attention to Him. (By the way, that self-proclaimed "Christ" in the newspaper ad never did show up.)

Most important of all, if you're a Christian, you won't miss His coming. You'll be returning to earth *with* Him! All the believers on earth will be raptured before the Tribulation, and taken up to heaven while God's judgment is poured out upon the earth. Then at the end of the Tribulation, Jesus will descend from heaven on a white horse to destroy all His enemies and set up His millennial kingdom. "And the armies in heaven, clothed in fine linen, white and clean, followed Him on white horses" (Revelation 19:14). We will be among "the armies in heaven" who come to earth with Jesus to live and reign with Him. What a glorious day that will be!

Our citizenship is in heaven, from which we also eagerly wait for the Savior, the Lord Jesus Christ, who will transform our lowly body that it may be conformed to His glorious body....

PHILIPPIANS 3:20-21

WELCOME HOME!

*My whole outlook upon everything that happens
to me should be governed by these three things:
my realization of who I am, my consciousness of
where I am going, and my knowledge of
what awaits me when I get there.*

D. MARTYN LLOYD-JONES

TRULY, THERE IS NO PLACE LIKE HOME. Jerry and I have both traveled widely, and the comforts of home are especially missed when you're in a foreign country. When the culture and customs are so different that you feel terribly out of place, when there's a language barrier and you can't communicate with anyone, and when you have nowhere to turn if something goes wrong, you come to appreciate the familiarity of home all the more. A citizen always feels welcome in his or her home country, which is a safe port of refuge in the midst of a chaotic and dangerous world.

Now, according to the apostle Paul, if you're a Christian, you're a citizen of heaven. That's your real home. Indeed, if you've been a believer any length of time, you may have come to feel as if, here on earth, you're a traveler in a foreign country. We live in a world that holds to different values, that doesn't speak the same language in a spiritual sense, and that even persecutes Christians. Some of us are ostracized in the workplace and our kids are ridiculed at school. We find ourselves repulsed by sin, whereas those who are citizens of this world freely indulge in it. And while modern-day society vigorously promotes the idea of tolerance toward all, it's clear that many of these advocates of tolerance are actually intolerant of Christians.

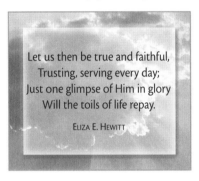

Let us then be true and faithful,
Trusting, serving every day;
Just one glimpse of Him in glory
Will the toils of life repay.

ELIZA E. HEWITT

These are just a few of the reasons we can look forward to heaven. There, we will feel welcomed and fit right in with everything around us. We will know the fullness of our status as children of God and enjoy a freedom of worship that is unhindered by societal or governmental constraints. God will be both our Father and our ruler. We will feel comfortable and relaxed because the kingdom we live in will be perfect and just. We won't have to deal with the agony and frustration of being surrounded by temptation, sin, injustice, and intolerance.

And the good news doesn't stop there. Not only will our *surroundings* change, but our *bodies* will change as well! Right after reminding us that we are citizens of heaven, Paul goes on to say that the Lord Jesus Christ "will transform our lowly body that it may be conformed to His glorious body" (Philippians 3:21).

That's going to be quite a transformation. Every impairment and problem we know in our physical bodies here on earth will be completely removed. We'll have no more tiredness, no more sickness, no more disabilities. The sting of terminal illness and death will be forever gone. Every effect and influence of sin will be totally eradicated. We will enjoy perfect health in glorious bodies. When the Lord raptures us to heaven, our corruptible and mortal bodies will become incorruptible and immortal (1 Corinthians 15:53-54), and we will dwell with the Lord forever and ever.

The hope of heaven under troubles is like wind and sails to the soul.

SAMUEL RUTHERFORD

Do you live each day with an awareness that you're a citizen of heaven? And that your weak body will one day become glorious? These truths are wonderful reminders of the great hope we have as Christians. In using the word *hope*, we're not saying that we are merely hoping that we will make it to heaven and that our bodies will be made perfect. Ours is a hope that is absolutely certain and cannot be taken away from us.

So whenever you get discouraged about how difficult it is to live as a Christian in this world, or whenever you become frustrated by your body's limitations, remember Philippians 3:20-21, and remind yourself of the hope you have as a believer. God Himself has promised and reserved for you a place in His future kingdom—a place in which you will have a perfect home and perfect body.

So when this corruptible has put on
incorruption, and this mortal has put on
immortality, then shall be brought to
pass the saying that is written: "Death is
swallowed up in victory."

1 Corinthians 15:54

GOD'S AWESOME POWER OVER DEATH

*Jesus has transformed death
from a dreary cavern into
a passage leading to glory.*

CHARLES SPURGEON

A SKEPTIC ONCE ASKED ME, "How is a Christian sailor buried at sea going to be resurrected?" Before I could answer he jeeringly added, "Suppose his body is eaten by a fish, which in turn is caught by fishermen and brought to a cannery where it is processed, then eaten by humans? How will God ever resurrect that sailor's body?"

Like most skeptics, his concept of God was too small. While the ways of God are "past finding out" (Romans 11:33), we do have some insights on how such a resurrection might take place. Consider the many Christian martyrs whose bones and flesh were destroyed by fire and the elements of their bodies seemingly lost to the smoke. The future resurrection will include their bodies, as well as the bodies of those who, buried centuries ago, have long since decomposed into dust. Indeed, no matter how radical the form of decomposition, *every* Christian's body will be raised at the resurrection.

God is powerful enough to take care of this problem. But for those who must have some sort of scientific explanation, let us remember this: matter is neither created nor destroyed. While a body may turn to dust or ashes, the elements of that person will never leave the universe. It will be simple for God—who created the entire universe out of nothing!—to call together the elements of all the people who have ever lived, and raise them in a new resurrected form. Millions of Christians have died through the ages, but our infinite and omnipotent God is able to keep track of all their elements and will reassemble them on Resurrection Day. If He was able to speak this complex and intricate world into existence, then He will be able to bring us back to life in a new and improved form.

> He is coming, our Lord and Master,
> Our Redeemer and King;
> We shall see Him in all His beauty,
> And His praise we shall sing.
> He shall gather His chosen people,
> Who are called by His name;
> And the ransomed of every nation
> For His own He shall claim.
>
> FANNY CROSBY

The apostle Paul refers to our present "corruptible" body being "changed—in a moment, in the twinkling of an eye...and the dead [being] raised incorruptible" (1 Corinthians 15:51-52). On the day of our resurrection, the bodies of dead Christians and our degenerating bodies will all be transformed in a split second into perfect, glorious, incorruptible bodies.

So, death cannot keep us in the ground. That's why Paul says, "Death is swallowed up in victory" (verse 54). We have no reason to fear death. It's painful to know we will die one day and it hurts to lose a loved one to the grave. But for the Christian, death is only a temporary parting. At the very moment life ceases, a believer is immediately in the Lord's presence. And eventually, death will be forever destroyed, and we will all be reunited together in God's kingdom, never to be separated again.

The nearer I approach the end, the plainer I hear around me the immortal symphonies which invite me.

VICTOR HUGO

Isn't that a wonderful assurance, an encouraging hope to have? To realize we have no reason to fear death? We live in a world that has long searched for the secret to immortality. Many ancient peoples believed that if they followed certain rituals, they could increase the chances of their loved ones reaching the afterlife. And today, medical researchers work zealously to extend our lifespan and even freeze dead bodies in the hope we'll be able to bring them back to life someday. But all this is in vain. Only the Lord Jesus Christ has conquered death—and He is the "firstfruits of those who have fallen asleep" (1 Corinthians 15:20). Because He rose from the dead, we know that through His power, we too will rise from the dead.

This concept of resurrection gives us a bit more appreciation for all that Jesus did on the cross. It was there He paid the debt for our sin, taking our judgment on Himself in order to give us eternal life. It also increases our anticipation of Christ's calling us home at the rapture. After that, "we shall always be with the Lord" (1 Thessalonians 4:17). Then our victory will be complete!

*N*ow, brethren, concerning the
coming of our Lord Jesus Christ and our
gathering together to Him, we ask you,
not to be soon shaken in mind or
troubled, either by spirit or by word
or by letter, as if from us, as though
the day of Christ had come.

2 THESSALONIANS 2:1-2

DON'T LET OTHERS
STEAL YOUR HOPE

*The supreme hope of seeing
Christ is a hope that will never,
never be disappointed.*

R. W. FORREST

Y EARS AGO, A NORTH CAROLINA FISHERMAN found a fairly large rock in a stream where he was fishing and took it to his cabin home. Not having a mantel over his fireplace on which to place it, he used it as a doorstop. Years later, a geologist was hiking through the area and the man invited him in for coffee. The gesture turned out to be extremely profitable. As his guest began examining the rock, he found it was solid gold. In fact, it turned out to be the largest chunk of gold ever found east of Colorado.

To many Christians, the second coming is like that lump of gold. It is a valuable doctrine mentioned in all the creeds of Christendom and in the doctrinal statements of most churches, but in too many of these churches it is ignored. In fact, in the course of traveling and meeting people in connection with the Left Behind series, Jerry and I have met a number of pastors who avoid teaching about the second coming because they're afraid of confusing people who don't know anything about the last days, and they're concerned they might inadvertently cause disagreements to surface among members of their congregations. As a result, the teaching of Christ's return—and the practical effects it can have—ends up having little or no place in many people's lives. It is gold unrecognized and unclaimed.

> Is all this something that should frighten us? Excited, yes. Frightened, no. What could be more exciting and encouraging than the idea that some of us will never die?
>
> JACK VAN IMPE

Considering that the return of Christ is the second-most-frequently mentioned doctrine in the Bible, it should hold a place of great importance in our lives. As we talked about earlier in this book, living in the awareness of our Lord's soon return should have a profound effect on us, motivating us toward holiness, inspiring us to evangelize to the lost, and giving us a greater appreciation for world missions.

When pastors and Christians admit to ignoring the second coming because it's a fearful subject, Jerry and I remind them that Christ told us to *anticipate* His return, not *dread* it. Jesus Himself said of His coming, "Don't be troubled" (John 14:1). And in His masterful Olivet discourse in Matthew chapters 24–25, He warned His followers several times to beware of deceivers and false prophets and christs. He knew that Satan would do everything he could to cause believers to disregard sound teaching.

The little church in the ancient biblical city of Thessalonica was one place where Satan attempted to undermine the doctrine of the rapture. We read in 2 Thessalonians 2:2 that certain false teachers were troubling the Christians' confidence in the rapture "either by spirit or by word or by letter, as if from us" (Paul was evidently referring to a false letter probably written in his name). How better can Satan confuse and discourage congregations than to rob them of the contagious nature of the hope of Christ's return?

> The resurrection of Jesus Christ is our hope today. It is our assurance that we have a living Savior to help us live as we should now, and that when, in the end, we set forth on that last great journey, we shall not travel an uncharted course, but rather we shall go on a planned voyage—life to death to eternal living.
>
> RAYMOND MACKENDREE

Satan's attempts at confusion and deception still continue today. No one who takes the Bible literally questions the *fact* of Jesus' second coming. It is the *timing* of the event that Christians are disputing. What is the big question? When will Jesus come—before, in the middle of, or at the end of the Tribulation? Our study of end-times passages convinces us that our Lord will rapture His church before the Tribulation in which He will try the whole earth.

Some of our friends who believe the rapture will occur in the middle of or after the Tribulation like to tell us we should be warning Christians to get ready to go through the worst time the world has ever seen or will see—the Great Tribulation. Our response is always, "Why should we? God didn't!" There is not one Bible verse spoken by Jesus, Paul, or Peter that tells Christians they should prepare to endure the Tribulation. On the other hand, there *are* passages that promise we will be saved from the wrath to come. We won't be here when the Tribulation comes.

So don't be troubled over the timing of the rapture and then, subsequently, Christ's return. The rapture has not come, nor will it come, until Jesus shouts from heaven, calling His church home. When He does, we who believe will be out of here—instantly! We will leave the unbelieving world, which will go through the Tribulation.

Don't let anyone rob you of that hope!

*You have need of endurance,
so that after you have done
the will of God, you may receive
the promise: "For yet a little while,
and He who is coming will come
and will not tarry."*

HEBREWS 10:36-37

WHILE
WE WAIT

'Mid toil and tribulation, and tumult of her war,
She waits the consummation of peace forevermore;
Till with the vision glorious her longing eyes are blest,
And the great church victorious shall be the church at rest.

SAMUEL S. WESLEY

Lord, HURRY UP AND GIVE ME PATIENCE!" This has been my
(Tim) constant prayer. Patience is a virtue that I've always
found hard to wait on. All through my adolescence my
mother said, "Tim, when are you going to learn to be
patient?" During my three-month term at Moody Bible
Institute, before I joined the Air Force, my roommate
nagged me constantly, saying, "You need patience, Tim.
God has you where you are for a reason."

After the war I couldn't wait to be discharged and go
to college. Then when I met Beverly, I couldn't wait till
we got married. Then I fidgeted all through my university

schooling until I became a pastor. In fact, I started pastoring while only a junior in college. Through all this, I couldn't wait patiently. I was always looking ahead to whatever was next.

When I started memorizing Scripture en route to discipling men, I came upon a verse that has become a daily reminder for me to wait on the Lord. "You have need of endurance, so that after you have done the will of God, you may receive the promise" (Hebrews 10:36). The next verse connected this patience with the second coming by saying, "For yet a little while, and He who is coming will come and will not tarry" (verse 37).

> Consider the hourglass; there is nothing to be accomplished by rattling or shaking; you have to wait patiently until the sand, grain by grain, has run from one funnel into the other.
>
> JOHN MORGENSTERN

While we should be patient in all areas of life, we should especially wait patiently for Jesus' return, and waiting upon His coming should influence everything we do. Some might object, saying that Christians have been waiting for 2000 years and Jesus still has not returned. But the Bible says it's our responsibility to remain patient until He does come. The word "endurance" in Hebrews 10:36 can be translated "patience." Now, this doesn't mean we should dampen our enthusiasm and anticipation for Christ's second coming. Rather, we should never become overly anxious and lose our calm dependency as we yearn for Him. We should simply live each day expecting it to be the day, knowing it's possible that it might be the day of His return.

An excellent way to do this is to make the Bible a part of our daily lives. Just as we feed our physical body each day to give it energy and keep it healthy, we should feed our soul on "the bread of life" (John 6:35). The Word of God keeps the hope of Jesus' return alive in our hearts. Perhaps that is why God continually reminds us of the second coming all through the Bible, with more than 300 of those references in the New Testament alone.

It's when we fail to feed upon the Bible that we become spiritually malnourished—and end up becoming impatient or even apathetic about Jesus' return. Without our daily input from Scripture, we make ourselves vulnerable to Satan's discouragements, making us more prone to lose faith and turn away from the hope that is before us.

Some years ago, a friend of mine in the insurance business used to come to the church gym, and we would work out together two or three times a week during our lunch hours. We talked about everything. Gradually, as the church grew and my travels increased, our times together declined, and except for occasional meetings at church, we lost close touch with each other. About five years after I resigned my ministry at the church, I heard that on his fiftieth birthday this friend quit his job and left his wife, blaming his marital boredom on a midlife crisis. He brashly announced on his birthday that he needed "a new job, a new wife, and a new life"! When I heard this I remembered he was an avid reader of self-help and motivational books, but read very little from the Bible.

> But Jesus Christ is patient with us; when the hill is very steep He takes us up in His arms that we may get our breath again. But all this means expenditure of time, thought, care, solicitude; and all this means the exercise of a patience that cannot be fluttered, because it has its centre in eternity.
>
> JOSEPH PARKER

This friend has since had several jobs and multiple wives. He is living a miserable life because he has been feeding his soul on the wrong kind of information. Had he been reading the Psalms, the Gospels, or the epistles of Paul, he might have been challenged to personal righteousness and accountability by the many promises of the second coming. At one time I taught this friend how to keep a daily journal of God's blessings to him, but unfortunately, he quit that practice and replaced it with worldly pursuits.

God's Word has a way of prompting us and convicting us toward greater spiritual growth. And as we are reminded constantly by the truth that Jesus will indeed return, we become more motivated to live holy and build our treasures in heaven rather than upon earth. As Christians, we are called to a better hope. We are called to read the Word of God and stay focused as we patiently wait for Jesus' coming.

If the master returns and finds that the servant has done a good job, there will be a reward.

MATTHEW 24:46 NLT

*O*ccupy till I come.

LUKE 19:13 KJV

Bringing the Blessed Hope to Others

*God does not ask about our ability
or our inability, but our availability.*

AUTHOR UNKNOWN

Have you ever heard of the malady known as evangelitis? What about servantitus? Perhaps you haven't been introduced to these afflictions before, but you've experienced the symptoms firsthand. *Evangelitis* includes becoming nervous about mentioning anything about the Bible or Christ to an unbeliever. It's usually accompanied by a persistent phobia of praying in public and being seen with a Bible or Christian book in your hand. Also, in your heart you pray for loved ones or close friends to come to Christ, but you also pray that God will use someone else to make it happen, rather than yourself.

"I'm not very good at talking about spiritual matters" is the disclaimer we give when we are enfeebled by evangelitis. "My mind simply goes blank."

Servantitus is marked by a fear or reluctance to serve in the church in some capacity—*any* capacity. Sometimes we don't recognize we have this ailment because, at first glance, we think our problem is a lack of time. "I have so many other obligations I wouldn't be able to help out anyway." Or, we assume we're not needed, saying, "There are plenty of other people available to do the work." And then there was Moses' own version of servantitus, which says, "I don't have what it takes. I don't have the necessary skills. Please, Lord, find someone else to do the job."

> If we are faithful to God in little things, we shall gain experience and strength that will be helpful to us in the more serious trials of life.
>
> HUDSON TAYLOR

These kinds of responses grieve the Lord's heart. He actually finds pleasure in working through us, and He can work through anyone, including you. There are all kinds of ways you can serve Him—not only in your church, but in your home, your friendships with other believers, and even your neighborhood and workplace.

In Luke 19, Jesus taught that we are to "occupy till I come." Notice that in the parable of the talents in Matthew 25:14-30, the Master (representing Jesus) gave different amounts of money to different servants. One was given a lot, one was given a moderate amount, and one was given a little. Jesus has done the same to us, and all He asks is that we make use of what He has entrusted to us, rather than neglect it. And remember that God promises to empower us—He doesn't leave us on our own. This empowerment is mentioned in both Ephesians 3:20 ("Now to Him who is able

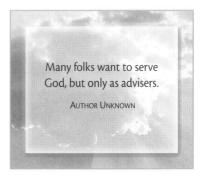

Many folks want to serve God, but only as advisers.

AUTHOR UNKNOWN

to do exceedingly abundantly above all that we ask or think, *according to the power that works in us"*) and Philippians 4:13 ("I can do *all things through Christ* who strengthens me").

Ultimately, serving Christ while we wait for His return has nothing to do with our ability or inability. Rather, it has everything to do with *availability.* Let me share two stories of people who simply made themselves available…and who, in direct and indirect ways, brought hope to other lives.

Dr. George W. Truett, pastor of the First Baptist Church of Dallas, tells of a prominent, unbelieving doctor in that city who regularly attended one of the church's Sunday morning services with his Christian wife. On this particular Sunday they were seated in the front row of the balcony. During the invitation the pastor grimaced as he saw a 12-year-old, mentally retarded girl go to the doctor and begin talking to him. Dr. Truett groaned, believing that this little girl—known to be an outspoken witness for Christ—would probably turn the doctor off. But a brief one stanza later, the doctor, who had been the object of many prayers, came forward to receive Christ.

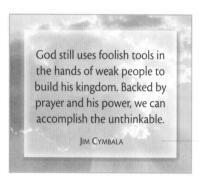

God still uses foolish tools in the hands of weak people to build his kingdom. Backed by prayer and his power, we can accomplish the unthinkable.

JIM CYMBALA

As they were leaving the church that Sunday, the pastor asked the physician what it was that caused him to come forward. The doctor said, "It was what little Millie said to me. You see, she has been my patient her entire life. From birth we knew that she would be mentally retarded, but I have grown to love her and she, me. After your sermon she was so concerned for my soul, she came over and said to me, 'Doctor, do you want to go to heaven with us?' I replied, 'No!' Then she sadly responded, 'Then you will have to go to hell.' Suddenly I realized she was right. If I did not receive Jesus I would be eternally lost. I owe my conversion to Millie's gentle frankness."

Millie could never teach a Sunday school class, preach a sermon, or even give her testimony in public. But she was a bold witness for her Lord and did not hesitate to urge all she knew to accept the Savior.

Then there was the carpenter who attended the first church I pastored, located in Minnesota. One cold winter day, he and I were the only people in the church. He was putting up wallboard in the gymnasium. From the warm office where I sat, I could hear him pounding at his work. I went down to talk to him and found him wearing wool gloves. When I asked why he was working on such a cold day, he said, "Pastor, I can't teach a Sunday school class, but I can build rooms where someone else can do it. I am working here to invest in something eternal." That was almost 45 years ago. That workman has been in heaven for many years now, but his works still bear fruit here on earth. Recently I visited that church building and stopped in that same Sunday school room. There were at least 70 junior-aged boys and girls learning about Jesus. The carpenter's labors had not been in vain.

It's to people like Millie and the carpenter whom the Lord will say, "Well done, my good and faithful servant. Enter into the joy of your Lord." Not because they did anything that, by human standards, would be considered great. But simply because they made themselves available. They yielded themselves to God, and God used them. That's all God asks from each of us.

$\mathcal{T}$he Lord is…longsuffering toward us, not willing that any should perish but that all should come to repentance.

2 Peter 3:9

THE GOD OF MANY CHANCES

Strange as this may sound to you, this is God's final effort to get the attention of every person who has ignored or rejected him. He is allowing now a vast period of trial and tribulation to come to you who remain. He has removed his church from a corrupt world that seeks its own way, its own pleasures, its own ends. I believe God's purpose in this is to allow those who remain to take stock of themselves and leave their frantic search for pleasure and self-fulfillment, and turn to the Bible for truth and to Christ for salvation.[1]

LEFT BEHIND

IN OUR NOVEL *LEFT BEHIND,* those were the words spoken by a pastor who created a videotape intended for those who missed the rapture. This pastor knew that after the rapture, many on earth would wonder what was going on. Where did the missing people go? Why were so many cataclysmic disasters taking place? Did those who were left behind still have any hope of getting to heaven?

You may have found yourself asking that last question about your unsaved family members and friends. You may have wondered, *Lord, after all the Christians are raptured, will the unbelievers whom I care about still have a chance? Is there any hope that they'll somehow hear the gospel message and become saved?* Such concern is understandable. All of us know people whom we love and whom we grieve for because we know that without salvation in Christ, they won't go to heaven.

> When the trumpet of the Lord shall sound,
> and time shall be no more,
> And the morning breaks, eternal, bright, and fair;
> When the saved of earth shall gather over on the other shore,
> And the roll is called up yonder, I'll be there.
>
> JAMES M. BLACK

The good news is yes, they will get another chance. In fact, they will have multiple opportunities. That doesn't guarantee they will accept Christ as their Savior and Lord, but they will definitely have the opportunity to do so. God even provides for us, in the book of Revelation, a sneak preview of these "second chances."

The Two Witnesses

Among the most colorful characters in all the Bible are the two supernatural prophets who will burst on the scene during the first 1,260 days of the Tribulation (Revelation 11:3-4). God calls them "My two witnesses."

They will dress in sackcloth, proclaim prophecies, dispense astonishing miracles, and witness to the grace of God in a hostile environment in the city of Jerusalem.

These witnesses will preach repentance, among other things, leading many people to Christ. Their miracles will affirm their power is from God, and even the Antichrist will not be able to get rid of them until God's appointed time for that to happen. The fact that we live in the electronic age assures the message of these two witnesses will be broadcast worldwide via television, radio, and the Internet.

The 144,000 Jewish Witnesses

One of Jesus' best-known promises about the end of the age is found in Matthew 24:14: "This gospel of the kingdom will be preached in *all* the world as a witness to *all* the nations, and then the end will come." This is mentioned in the context of Christ's teaching on the last days. So we can be certain that a significant part of this preaching of the gospel will be accomplished through the ministry of the 144,000 witnesses described in Revelation 7, who reach "a great multitude which no one could number, of all nations, tribes, peoples, and tongues" (verse 9). We know these witnesses are Jewish, for they were "of all the tribes of Israel" (verse 4).

So, God will raise up an army of 144,000 Jewish evangelists to spread across the globe and bring in a soul harvest of unimaginable proportions.

Angel with the Everlasting Gospel

Remarkably, everyone who is alive at a certain point during the seven-year Tribulation is guaranteed to hear the gospel message. In Revelation 14:6-7 we read, "Then I saw another angel flying in the midst of heaven, having the everlasting gospel to preach to those who dwell on the earth—to every nation, tribe, tongue, and people—saying with a loud voice, 'Fear God and give glory to Him, for the hour of His judgment has come; and worship Him who made heaven and earth, the sea and springs of water.'"

This angel will somehow bring the gospel to all peoples of all nations. Everyone will have a chance to make a decision. And, as we can expect, some will accept Christ, while others will reject Him.

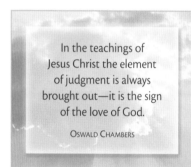

In the teachings of Jesus Christ the element of judgment is always brought out—it is the sign of the love of God.

Oswald Chambers

Yes, the number of people who become Christians during the soul harvest will be too great to count (Revelation 7:1). Will your loved ones and friends be among them? There's no way of knowing. What we *can* know is this: God is a merciful God. He waits patiently, not desiring that anyone would perish (2 Peter 3:9). He will give plenty of opportunities for people to receive salvation in Christ during the Tribulation. This time period will be the "final call," and it will be a well-proclaimed call at that. God's desire is for a maximum number of souls to become saved, and that's why He has waited for so long before bringing final judgment upon this world.

We have a God who will go to incredible lengths to bring people to Himself.

God *also has highly exalted Him*
and given Him the name which
is above every name, that at
the name of Jesus every knee should
bow, of those in heaven, and
of those on earth, and of those under
the earth, and that every tongue
should confess that Jesus Christ is Lord,
to the glory of God the Father.

PHILIPPIANS 2:9-11

EVERY KNEE WILL BOW

Worship is the declaration
by a creature of the
greatness of his Creator.

HERBERT M. CARSON

DOES YOUR HEART GRIEVE WHEN YOU SEE disrespect or mockery directed at Jesus Christ?

That's probably the case when you hear Jesus' name used in vain. Or when, on television or in a movie, Christ is portrayed in some negative or demeaning way. At the workplace we may overhear our coworkers spouting derogatory jokes about Jesus, and in school classrooms, our children may hear ridicule directed at Christians and the church—ridicule that ultimately shows disregard for the Lord Jesus.

And nothing can compare with the derision and scorn that was hurled at Jesus during His trials and crucifixion. He who is the embodiment of truth was called a liar. He was charged with crimes He never committed. The officials presiding at His trials broke many of the rules of legal procedure in both Roman and Jewish courts. So great was the hatred directed toward Jesus that even when the Roman governor Pilate could find no wrong done by Him, the religious leaders and people demanded He be put to death. He was cruelly scourged with a whip, mocked with a crown of thorns and a purple robe, and brutally hit and spat upon. Then this perfectly righteous and innocent Lamb of God was punished by crucifixion, a sentence reserved only for the most despicable and wretched of criminals.

> Let every kindred, every tribe,
> On this terrestrial ball,
> To Him all majesty ascribe,
> And crown Him Lord of all.
>
> EDWARD PERRONET

In the 2000 years since, countless people have continued to dishonor the Lord Jesus Christ. Sometimes the offense is subtle, other times it's flagrant. Sometimes it's done more out of ignorance, other times it's deliberate and malicious. But no matter what the severity of or the reason for the disrespect, ultimately, it reflects a heart rebellious against God. When we who are Christians witness such disregard, we cannot help but feel hurt. In fact, we may wonder, *Lord, how can You take all this? Why don't you put these people in their place? How can you, as the King of kings and Lord of lords, show such great patience in the face of the world's contempt?*

There is coming a day, however, when all this will change.

When Christ returns, it will be in power and great glory. He will completely subdue His enemies, set up His kingdom on earth, and rule for all eternity. In the end, every knee will bow and every tongue will confess that Jesus Christ is Lord (Philippians 2:10-11). More specifically, verse 10 says that every knee "in heaven and on earth and *under* the earth" will bow (NIV). Every single living being who refused to pay homage to Jesus through the ages—including Satan himself—will finally be forced to confess Him as Lord of all. They will not make this confession willingly, but out of terror, knowing that their eternal condemnation rests in Christ's hands. At the Great White Throne Judgment, they will be "judged according

> God is working His purpose out
> as year succeeds to year,
> God is working His purpose out
> and the time is drawing near;
> Nearer and nearer draws the
> time, the time that shall surely be,
> When the earth shall be filled
> with the glory of God
> as the waters cover the sea.
>
> ARTHUR CAMPBELL AINGER

to what he had done" and then "thrown into the lake of fire" (Revelation 20:13,15 NIV).

From then onward, those of us who have willingly bowed our knee in reverence to Christ will join with the heavenly host in declaring praises and honor to Him. We will have the privilege and joy of seeing our Lord glorified as He should be. He will have His rightful place not only on the throne of our hearts, but on a physical throne that marks His authority and rule over all creation. And we will reign together with Him forever and ever.

With such a wonderful future ahead of us, it's no wonder the apostle John closed the book of Revelation by exuberantly proclaiming, "Even so, come, Lord Jesus!"

*A*nd I saw a new heaven and
a new earth, for the first heaven and the
first earth had passed away.

REVELATION 21:1

How Will
It End?

*Enemy-occupied territory—
that is what the world is.*

C. S. Lewis

In recent decades, more and more scholars, authors, journalists, and even people on the street have been making increasingly frequent use of the expression *the end of history*. Their use of the term is often a reflection of their doomsday view of the geopolitical landscape. We are, as some say, the most educated generation in all history. Yet measured by the number of wars and deaths in the last century, we are also quite likely the most barbaric generation. It is estimated that approximately 180 million people have been killed by their fellow human beings in this century alone.

Any honest historian can see that this world is on a collision course with annihilation. Germ warfare and the existence of nuclear bombs make this world a frightening planet to call home. Considering the possibility that such weapons are still proliferating and could be misused by unstable governments or by terrorists, it's no wonder so many people have a hard time being hopeful about the future.

> Do you feel no sacred passion stirring your breast to anguish for the present, and to hope for the future? O ye cravens, who dread the battle, slink to your beds; but ye who have your Master's spirit in you, and would long to see brighter and better days, lift up your heads with confidence in him who will walk with us if we be agreed.
>
> CHARLES SPURGEON

We who are Christians, however, have an inside track on the future. We have what the apostle Peter calls a "sure word of prophecy" (KJV) to guide us. This Word paints for us an optimistic picture that gives us every reason to be confident. The world is not going to be destroyed by man. Yes, we will still see some difficult times in the ugly continuum of humanity's inhumanity. And yes, the world will continue its downward spiral into depravity, with people being "lovers of themselves...unholy, unloving, unforgiving, without self-control, brutal, despisers of good" (2 Timothy 3:2-3). But we're not going to destroy the earth.

God has revealed in His prophetic Word that He has great plans for this world and all who live in it. After the rapture of the church, many people will still be present on this earth. Many of them will follow the Antichrist and, ultimately, reject God. Yet "a great multitude, which no one could number, of all nations, tribes, peoples, and tongues" (Revelation 7:9), will repent of their sin and turn to Christ for salvation.

> The motto of our hope is not the "perhaps" which is the most that it can say when it speaks the tongue of earth, but the "verily! verily!" which comes to its enfranchised lips when it speaks the tongue of heaven.
>
> ALEXANDER MACLAREN

Even with all the unfathomably horrible judgments that will take place during the Tribulation, people will still survive, as will the earth. Following the Tribulation, Jesus will judge the nations and begin His kingdom—right here on the earth. Revelation chapter 20 states no less than six times that this kingdom will last 1000 years.

As for the earth, nothing will happen to it until after Jesus' 1000-year kingdom comes to an end. At that time will come the Great White Throne Judgment, at which Christ will judge all unbelievers from all the ages and send them to eternal condemnation. This judgment is described at the end of Revelation 20. Right after that, in the very first verse of Revelation chapter 21, we read that God will bring forth "a new heaven and a new earth."

So, for Christians, the future is very bright. No matter what the doomsayers say, we will not destroy this earth. Instead, the Lord Jesus Christ will come here to establish His millennial kingdom, which will be free of the wars and hatred and destruction that are so rampant today. And then at the end of the millennial kingdom, God will do away with the old earth and create a new one.

Are you ready for that? If you're a Christian, this will be a glorious time. But if you aren't, now is the time to call on the name of the Lord and be saved. He paid the price of your salvation. It comes at no cost to you. You have but to receive it. Receive this gift and join God's children at the rapture. You need not be left behind when Jesus comes to claim His church.

Surely goodness and mercy shall
follow me all the days
of my life; and I will dwell in
the house of the LORD *forever.*

PSALM 23:6

THE BEST IS
YET TO COME!

How ravishing will be the joys of the redeemed in the mansions of glory! What ineffable joy will fill the soul of the believer, when he sits down with Abraham, Isaac, and Jacob, in the kingdom of God—when he reigns with Immanuel on his throne—when he views all heaven's bliss as his. Amidst such joys as these, surely his enraptured soul must be lost in wonder, love, and praise.

D. A. HARSHA

How do you describe eternity? How can you begin to picture an unending moment of happiness and contentment and joy in the presence of an eternally smiling God?

The psalmist wrote, "In Your presence is fullness of joy" (Psalm 16:11). The joy we experience in heaven will be far beyond anything we've ever known here on earth. Consider what author D. A. Harsha wrote about this joy in a book written more than 100 years ago:

When the Christian has passed the vale of life, and done with mortal care and grief, the Saviour will welcome him home to glory with this joyful invitation, "Enter thou into the joy of thy Lord." Then begins the heavenly joy of the believer. He rests with Jesus; he enters into the joy of his Lord. And what is this joy? What is there about it that is so attractive? It is a joy unspeakable and full of glory. The pen cannot describe it, nor the tongue declare it. It is the joy of being with Christ—the joy of possessing the heavenly inheritance—a fullness of joy. The joy of heaven is full, satisfying, and eternal. It is ecstatic joy. It transports the ransomed soul with ineffable delights.[2]

Yes, heaven is going to be wonderful. We get our most expansive peek into what this realm will be like in Revelation chapters 21–22, where the apostle John sets the stage with these words:

I saw a new heaven and a new earth, for the first heaven and the first earth had passed away. Also there was no more sea. Then I, John, saw the holy city, New Jerusalem, coming down out of heaven from God, prepared as a bride adorned for her husband. And I heard a loud voice from heaven saying, "Behold, the tabernacle of God is with men, and He will dwell with them, and they shall be

His people, and God Himself will be with them and be their God. And God will wipe away every tear from their eyes; there shall be no more death, nor sorrow, nor crying; and there shall be no more pain, for the former things have passed away" (Revelation 21:1-4).

What a place God has prepared for us from before the foundation of the world! John spotlights for us the best part of any description of eternity when he writes that God Himself will live with us, and we will be His people. What a wonder this will be—to continually see God's face (Revelation 22:4) and to walk in the light of His presence (21:23; 22:5)!

As we read Revelation 21–22, we notice there are a number of things we won't find in heaven:

- no more sea (21:1)
- no more tears, death, sorrow, crying, or pain (21:4)
- no more sinners (21:8)
- no more fear (21:12)
- no more sun or moon (21:23)
- no more night (21:25)
- no more sin or evil (21:27)
- no more disease or injuries (22:2)
- no more curse (22:3)

It would be enough to call this place heaven just from the list of what it lacks. But that wouldn't tell the half of the story! Now consider some of the remarkable features we will enjoy in eternity:

- unending fellowship with God (21:3,7,22)
- unending newness (21:5)
- unending water of life (21:6; 22:1)
- unimaginable beauty (21:11,21)
- unbroken unity between believers (21:12,14)
- unlimited holiness (21:16)
- untold wealth (21:18-21)
- unending light (21:23; 22:5)
- unceasing service to God (22:3)
- unending reign (22:5)

Indeed, God has prepared a place for us that is beyond our wildest imaginations. John the apostle and the other Bible writers could only hint at its true wonder, for the only way to fully appreciate the place will be to experience it personally. And we know only a small fraction of what God has in store for the future—"eye has not seen, nor ear heard, nor have entered into the heart of man the things which God has prepared for those who love Him" (1 Corinthians 2:9).

This is going to be our dwelling place for *eternity!* Isn't that mind-boggling? And it's all being given to us as a free gift by God Himself. Does that give you a greater sense for just *how much* He loves us? He paid an infinitely incalculable price when He sent His Son to the cross to redeem us from our sin. His pain was our gain. He made it all possible. As a result, we who are His children have an indescribably wonderful destiny ahead of us.

> When we've been there
> ten thousand years,
> Bright shining as the sun,
> We've no less days
> to sing God's praise
> Than when we first begun.
>
> JOHN NEWTON

Yes, the best is yet to come!

NOTES

1. Tim LaHaye and Jerry B. Jenkins, *Left Behind* (Wheaton, IL: Tyndale House Publishers, 1995), p. 212.

2. D.A. Harsha, *The Heavenly Token* (New York: H. Dayton, Publisher, 1859), pp. 447-448.

OTHER GOOD READING

Tim LaHaye and Jerry B. Jenkins

God Always Keeps His Promises. The bestselling *LEFT BEHIND®
SERIES* is the inspiration for this gift book celebrating the ultimate
promise of God—the gift of His Son, Jesus Christ. An encouraging
collection of First Coming prophecy Scriptures and their fulfillment.

Are We Living in the End Times? The biblical foundation for the *LEFT
BEHIND® SERIES* of novels (Tyndale House Publishers).

Perhaps Today: Living in the Light of Christ's Return. A ninety-day
devotional treatment of Second Coming Scriptures that is both
instructive and inspirational (Tyndale House Publishers).

THE LEFT BEHIND® SERIES. Eleven exciting novels based on the
prophetic Scriptures (Tyndale House Publishers).

The Promise of Heaven. An inspiring collection of Scriptures, classic
quotes, and personal prayers and writings in a beautifully decorated
volume (Harvest House Publishers).

Tim LaHaye and Thomas Ice

Charting the End Times. This visual resource of charts and
well–written explanatory text provides a fascinating picture of the
times ahead (Harvest House Publishers).

Charting the End Times Prophecy Study Guide. An interactive study
about the Rapture, the Tribulation, the return of Christ, the judgment, the Millennial kingdom, heaven, and more (Harvest House
Publishers).

For more information on these and other great books, visit

www.leftbehind.com
www.tyndale.com
www.harvesthousepublishers.com